MINERALS

Chris Oxlade

Peachtree

Edited by Helen Cox Cannons
Designed by Philippa Jenkins
Original illustrations © Capstone Global Library Limited 2016
Picture research by Tracy Cummins
Production by Victoria Fitzgerald
Originated by Capstone Global Library Limited
Printed and bound in China

19 18 17 16 15
10 9 8 7 6 5 4 3 2 1

Library of Congress Cataloging-in-Publication Data
Cataloging-in-publication information is on file with the Library of Congress.
ISBN 978-1-4109-8137-0 (library binding)
ISBN 978-1-4109-8145-5 (eBook PDF)

Acknowledgments
The author and publisher are grateful to the following for permission to reproduce copyright material: Alamy: Stocktrek Images, Inc., 22; Capstone Press: Karon Dubke, 28, 29, Getty Images: DEA PICTURE LIBRARY, 27; iStockphoto: laurent, 19, PhilipCacka, 21; Newscom: YOUTH JIN/FEATURECHINA, 11; Science Source: Dirk Wiersma, 17, Millard H. Sharp, 12, Scimat, 23 Left; Shutterstock: Albert Russ, Cover, 1, 4, AndiPu, 10, Bokic Bojan, 14, Bragin Alexey, 6, Coffeemill, 5, CREATISTA, 26, gvictoria, 23 Right, Imfoto, 16, Jiri Vaclavek, 8, Kotomiti Okuma, 25, Mironov56, 15, Olga Miltsova, 9, R3BV, 20, Santi Rodriguez, 13, Sergiy Kuzmin, 24 Bottom, Stellar Gems, 24 Top, Vlad Teodor, 18; Wikimedia: Alexander Van Driessche, 7.

The author would like to thank Dr. Gillian Fyfe for her invaluable help in the preparation of this book.

Every effort has been made to contact copyright holders of any material reproduced in this book. Any omissions will be rectified in subsequent printings if notice is given to the publisher.

All the Internet addresses (URLs) given in this book were valid at the time of going to press. However, due to the dynamic nature of the Internet, some addresses may have changed, or sites may have changed or ceased to exist since publication. While the author and publisher regret any inconvenience this may cause readers, no responsibility for any such changes can be accepted by either the author or the publisher.

Contents

Some words are shown in bold, **like this**. You can
find out what they mean by looking in the glossary.

What Are Minerals?

Minerals are natural, nonliving materials. They are found in the rocks of Earth's **crust** (the thin, rocky skin on the outside of Earth). That's because all rocks are made up of minerals. Most rocks are made of two, three, or more minerals mixed together.

The study of rocks is called geology, and the study of minerals is called mineralogy.

A scientist who studies geology is called a **geologist**. A scientist who studies minerals is called a **mineralogist**.

These are **crystals** of amethyst. They are a form of the mineral quartz.

⇒

Everyday Minerals

Even though minerals are found in rocks in the ground, we don't have to go searching for rocks to see them. We see minerals in lots of places in our everyday lives, often without realizing it.

The salt we put on our food is a mineral—it is called halite. The beautiful **gemstones** in jewelry, such as sapphires and emeralds, are minerals. Gold and silver are also minerals. Minerals are useful materials that we put to hundreds of different uses.

What Are Minerals Made of?

Minerals are made from substances called **elements**. An element is a substance that cannot be broken down into simpler substances by chemical reactions. Examples of elements are carbon, oxygen, and silicon. Some minerals are made of just one element, but most minerals are made of two or more elements together.

ROCK
SOLID
FACTS!

HOW MANY MINERALS?

Geologists have discovered more than 4,000 different minerals in the rocks of Earth's crust. They find around 100 new minerals each year.

What Do Minerals Look Like?

If you pick up a piece of rock, you can sometimes see pieces of different **minerals** in it. But sometimes the pieces are too small to see. Sometimes we find large pieces of minerals in rocks, in spaces in rocks, or in caves. Minerals come in a huge range of different colors and shapes.

The rock granite contains pieces of white quartz and pink feldspar.

Mineral Shapes

The pieces of minerals that we find in spaces in rocks, or in caves, are often beautiful **crystals**. Crystals have flat faces and straight edges. Most minerals form crystals, but some form other shapes. For example, the mineral hematite forms smooth, rounded lumps.

Growing Crystals

Crystals are made from tiny **particles**. The particles are too small to see, even with a very powerful microscope. There are billions and billions of particles in just one tiny crystal. The particles are joined in neat rows and columns. This is why crystals have flat faces and straight edges.

Crystals grow in liquids that contain particles of minerals. As the liquid cools or dries, the particles of the mineral clump together. They join firmly to each other, which causes a crystal to slowly grow.

ROCK SOLID FACTS!

GIANT CRYSTALS

Crystals can grow to an enormous size. The largest crystals ever found are in the Crystal Caves in Mexico. They are needle-shaped crystals of a mineral called gypsum. These crystals are up to 39 feet (12 meters) long and 6 feet (2 meters) thick.

Crystal Shapes

Minerals grow into **crystals** with different shapes and colors. For example, the salt mineral halite grows into crystals that are cubes. We say it has <u>cubic crystals</u>. The mineral beryl grows into crystals with six sides, like a six-sided pencil. We say it has <u>hexagonal crystals. Cubic and hexagonal are two crystal shapes.</u>

Minerals and Light

Minerals come in lots of different colors—browns, blues, greens, reds, golds, and silvers. Some minerals are white or completely colorless. **Geologists** sometimes crush a mineral into powder. The color of the powder of a mineral is called its streak. It helps geologists to find out which mineral it is.

The mineral garnet forms red or orange cubes.

MINERAL HARDNESS

Some minerals are hard and some are soft. Diamond is the hardest mineral. The mineral called talc is so soft you can crumble it with your fingers.

Mineralogists measure the hardness of a mineral on a scale called the Mohs scale. On the Mohs scale, 1 is very soft and 10 is very hard. Testing the hardness of a piece of mineral helps mineralogists to find out which mineral it is.

Luster

Luster is another **property** of minerals. Luster is how the surface of a mineral looks. It can be dull, shiny, silky, greasy, metallic, glassy, or sparkly.

Minerals can have different colors and luster.

Looking Through Minerals

Some minerals are *transparent*. This means they are see-through. Some minerals are *translucent*. This means you can see light coming through them, but you can't see right through them. Some minerals are *opaque*. This means you can't see through them at all.

Where Do We Find Minerals?

We find most **minerals** in the rocks of Earth's **crust**. There are three types of rock in Earth's crust: igneous rocks, sedimentary rocks, and metamorphic rocks.

- *Igneous rocks* are made when molten rock cools and hardens.
- *Sedimentary rocks* are formed from layers of **sediment**.
- *Metamorphic rocks* are made when other rocks are heated up or squeezed by huge forces.

All three of these types of rock are made from minerals.

Minerals are found in water and inside plants and animals (including humans). We also find minerals in places where we use them, such as building materials, ornaments, and jewelry.

The chalk in these cliffs is made from calcite.

Minerals in Sedimentary Rocks

Some sedimentary rocks are made from millions of shells and skeletons of **organisms** that lived in the sea. They are made from a mineral called calcite.

Other sedimentary rocks are made from pieces of old rocks that have been broken up by **erosion**. For example, sandstone is made from layers of sand, and most sand is made from quartz.

THE DEEPEST MINE

Miners sometimes have to dig far down to get to the minerals they want. The deepest mine ever dug is the TauTona gold mine in South Africa. One tunnel is 2.4 miles (3.9 kilometers) below the surface.

Sometimes useful minerals can be found near Earth's surface.

⟹

Minerals in Igneous and Metamorphic Rrocks

Igneous rocks are made when magma (molten rocks) cool. Minerals such as quartz and feldspar form as the magma turns to solid rock.

Metamorphic rocks are made when other rocks are heated up and squeezed by huge forces deep in Earth's crust. The minerals in the original rocks are often changed into new minerals during this process.

Minerals on Earth's Surface

You can find minerals where there are bare rocks on Earth's surface. These places include riverbeds, cliffs, mountains, and where roads are cut into land. You can also find pieces of minerals in soil.

Minerals in Spaces

Solid rocks contain tiny pieces of minerals joined together. But sometimes we find large **crystals** of minerals in cracks and holes in rocks or caves. These crystals grow when minerals **dissolved** in hot water flow through cracks, holes, and caves. This process can take thousands or millions of years.

Dissolved Minerals

If you've ever tasted seawater, you have found some minerals. The minerals are dissolved in the water—that's why seawater tastes salty. If you mix salt (the mineral halite) from the kitchen into a glass of water, you can see the salt slowly dissolve. The salt seems to disappear, but it doesn't really. It breaks up into tiny mineral **particles** that mix into the water.

 A geode is a rock cavity containing crystals.

HOW MUCH SALT IN THE SEA?

Every liter of seawater contains about 1.2 ounces (35 grams) of salt. That's a full tablespoon full. If all the world's oceans dried up, there would be enough salt left to make a crystal 164 miles (265 kilometers) across. It would be so large it would take you about two weeks to walk around it nonstop!

Minerals from Water

When water that has minerals in it dries up, you can see the minerals left behind. When salty water in a lake dries up, flat plains of salt are left behind. These are called salt lakes.

Stalactites and stalagmites in caves are made from a mineral called calcite. They form when water that contains dissolved calcite drips down from a cave roof.

Stalactites grow downward and stalagmites grow upward.

What Kinds of Minerals Are There?

Mineralogists organize **minerals** into different families. The minerals in each family are made up of similar **elements** (see page 5). Here are some of the most common minerals grouped by families. There are lots of guides to minerals in books and on the Internet, with photographs and lists of their **properties**.

Common Minerals

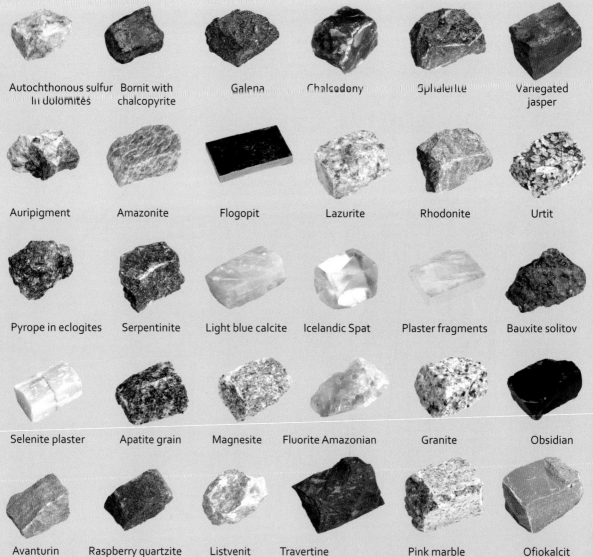

Autochthonous sulfur in dolomites	Bornit with chalcopyrite	Galena	Chalcedony	Sphalerite	Variegated jasper
Auripigment	Amazonite	Flogopit	Lazurite	Rhodonite	Urtit
Pyrope in eclogites	Serpentinite	Light blue calcite	Icelandic Spat	Plaster fragments	Bauxite solitov
Selenite plaster	Apatite grain	Magnesite	Fluorite Amazonian	Granite	Obsidian
Avanturin	Raspberry quartzite	Listvenit	Travertine	Pink marble	Ofiokalcit

This gold is in a vein of quartz.

Native Minerals

A native mineral is a mineral made up of just one element. Gold, silver, diamond, and sulfur are native minerals. Native minerals are found in their native form in rocks.

Gold and Silver

Gold is found in flakes, tiny grains, and pieces called nuggets. It is also found in veins of quartz and on quartz **crystals**. Gold is quite soft and **malleable** (easy to shape) and always stays shiny. Silver is found in wiry bunches or in tiny specks on rocks.

ROCK SOLID FACTS!

GOLD NUGGETS

Lumps of gold found in the ground or in rivers are called nuggets. The biggest nugget ever found was dug up in Australia in 1869. It was 24 inches (60 centimeters) long and weighed 159 pounds (72 kilograms). That's as heavy as an adult man!

Diamond

Diamond is made of the element carbon, so it is a native mineral. Diamond is made when rocks are heated and squeezed by immense forces in Earth's **crust**. It is the hardest of all minerals, so other minerals cannot scratch it.

Graphite

Graphite is also made of carbon, but it is very different from diamond. Pencil leads are made from graphite.

Oxide Minerals

An oxide **mineral** contains an **element** (normally a metal) combined with oxygen. Hematite is an oxide mineral and so is corundum. Rubies and sapphire are types of corundum.

Ruby is an oxide mineral.

⇨

Carbonate Minerals

A carbonate is a metal combined with carbon and oxygen. The most common carbonate mineral is calcium carbonate (also known as calcite). Chalk, limestone, and marble are made of calcite.

Sulfur Minerals

Sulfates and sulfide minerals are made up of a metal combined with sulfur, or sulfur and oxygen. Pyrite is made up of iron and sulfur. It is yellow and shiny. Pyrite is known as "fool's gold" because people sometimes mistake it for real gold. Gypsum is a very soft mineral made of calcium, oxygen, and sulfur.

A MAGNETIC MINERAL

The mineral magnetite is made from iron and oxygen. It is a magnetic mineral, so a piece of magnetite works as a magnet. If you hang a piece of magnetite on a string, it swings around like a compass needle does.

Silicate Minerals

Silicate minerals are often made with a metal combined with silicon and oxygen. The two most common minerals in Earth's **crust** are quartz and feldspar. Quartz makes up more than half of all rocks. Quartz comes in different types, such as milky quartz, rose quartz, amethyst, and smoky quartz. Agate, jasper, and onyx are types of quartz, too.

This is a mixture of quartz and feldspar **crystals**, which both contain silicon and oxygen.

Plants and animals need **minerals** to grow and to live. They get these minerals from the soil and the plants that grow in it.

If plants don't get the minerals they need, they cannot grow properly. If animals don't get all the minerals they need, they can become sick.

Minerals from the Soil

Soil is made up of pieces of rocks and minerals, together with pieces of rotting plants and living **organisms**. The water in soil also contains minerals in liquid form. Plants get minerals and water from the soil through their roots.

Adding Minerals

Some soils don't contain enough minerals for plants to grow properly. Plants that grow in these poor soils may grow slowly and have yellow leaves. At home, we can use plant food that contains minerals to make soil better. Farmers add **fertilizers** to their fields for the same reason.

Plant food contains the minerals that garden plants need to grow.

MINERAL TEETH AND BONES

Your teeth and bones are mainly made from a mineral called apatite. You need to drink milk when you are young because milk contains calcium, and your body needs calcium to make apatite.

Minerals from Food

All humans need iron to make our blood carry oxygen properly. Children need minerals such as calcium to build strong bones and teeth. You should get the minerals you need from eating a healthy, balanced diet made up of meat, fish, dairy foods, fruits, vegetables, and nuts.

A salt lick provides minerals for farm animals.

Where Do We Use Minerals?

We use hundreds of other **minerals** for thousands of different jobs. In this chapter, you can find out about where we use minerals in the form in which we find them.

Shiny Minerals

Gold, silver, and platinum are minerals that are shiny and **malleable**. "Malleable" means easy to bend and shape. They are all used for making jewelry, but they have many other uses, too. We make electrical connectors, such as headphone connectors, from gold. This is because gold **conducts** electricity very well. Silver is also used for electrical wires and for making batteries, ornaments, and trophies.

Gold is good for electrical contacts because it stays shiny.

A fire opal is set in a gold ring. ➡

...erals that
...s or patterns. They
...recious gemstones, such as
...lds, and sapphires, are also rare. We
use tr... ...elry, but they have many other uses,
too. For e... ...le, diamond is very tough and cannot be
scratched, so tiny, rough diamonds are glued to the tips
of drill bits. Semiprecious gemstones such as turquoise,
opal, and amethyst are also put into jewelry.

Ornamental Stones

Minerals such as jadeite, malachite, agate, and lapis
lazuli are not as precious as gemstones, but they come
in beautiful colors and patterns. They are often made
into ornaments.

ROCK SOLID FACTS!

RED DIAMONDS

Natural diamonds are valuable because they are rare.
The rarest natural diamonds are red diamonds. Only
around 20 of these beautiful gemstones have ever
been found. One of the largest red diamonds, called the
Kazanjian Diamond, is worth more than $50 million. It's
currently displayed at the American Museum of Natural
History in New York City.

Calcite

Calcite is the **mineral** that the rock limesto[ne]
Crushed-up calcite has lots of uses. Farmer[s]
their fields to make soil better for growing c[rops]
an ingredient in medicines such as indigestio[n]
in paints, and in cleaning products. Calcite is [in]
chicken food—it helps the chickens to produce

ROCK SOLID FACTS!

MINERAL MINES IN SPACE

Many minerals, such as platinum, are used to make the parts in gadgets such as computers and cell phones. These minerals are very rare on Earth. They are hard to find and also hard to get out of rocks. In the future, mining companies may try to get rare minerals from asteroids in space instead of from Earth's rocks.

This is an artist's impression of what a mining craft on an asteroid would look like.
⇒

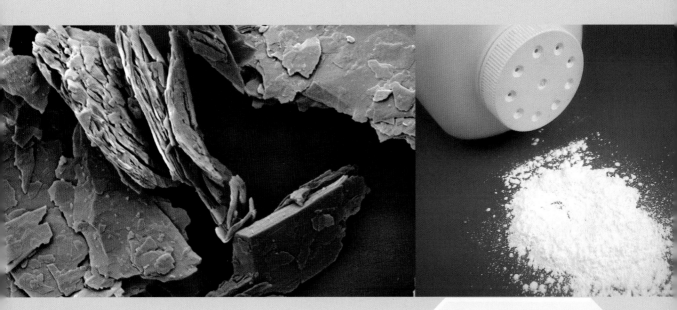

Halite

Halite is also called rock salt. We use rock salt for cooking and for treating icy roads to make the ice melt. Halite forms layers sometimes hundreds of feet thick in Earth's **crust**. We get it out by mining or by pumping water into the ground to **dissolve** it. Halite can also be rubbed into meat to stop the meat from going bad.

Talc

Talc is the softest of all minerals. Talc is ground down to make talcum powder. It is also used in paint and paper-making and in the manufacturing of rubber and plastic. Solid talc is sometimes called soapstone and is used for carving ornaments.

Graphite

Graphite is used to make batteries and the lead in pencils. It is also used to make the parts of machines slide more easily against each other.

What Materials Do We Get from Minerals?

Minerals are used in many different ways. In this chapter, you can find out about how we use minerals as raw materials. That means how we get materials from the minerals, and how we change the minerals into other materials.

Metals from Minerals

Many minerals contain metals such as iron and aluminum. We can get the metals out of the minerals and use them to make things. The minerals we get metals from are called metal ores.

We get iron from a mineral called hematite. Iron is the most important metal we use, because steel is a form of iron, and we make all sorts of things from steel. These things range from tiny nuts and bolts to enormous ships and skyscrapers.

Hematite

We get aluminum from bauxite, a rock that has important minerals. Aluminum is strong but lightweight. It is used to make objects from cooking pots and children's scooters to huge passenger aircraft.

Steel is made from iron extracted from hematite.

METALS BY ACCIDENT

About 6,000 years ago, humans discovered that they could get the metal copper from a mineral called malachite. Potters may have accidentally dropped malachite into hot fires and found copper in the ashes.

Getting Metals Out

It's not too difficult to dig mineral ores from the ground, but it's not easy to get metals out of the ores. The usual way of getting metals from ores is to heat up the ore until it melts. Then the metal flows out of the ore. This process is called smelting.

Copper is extracted from minerals such as chalcopyrite.

Building with Minerals

Some **minerals** are important raw materials for builders and engineers. Calcite is the main ingredient of cement.

<u>When cement is mixed with water and sand, it makes mortar. We use mortar to join bricks together in walls.</u>

<u>When cement is mixed with water, sand, and pieces of rock, it makes concrete.</u>

Gypsum is a similar mineral to calcite. Gypsum is the main ingredient in plaster and plasterboard.

Silica for Glass

The mineral silica is a very common mineral, because most sand is made of silica. Glass is made from silica. It is made by melting sand and mixing in a few other minerals, including calcite, and letting the mixture cool.

The chemical silicon comes from silica. The memory chips and other chips in computers and other electronic devices are made from silicon. So are solar cells and the sealants that builders put around windows, baths, and showers.

This man is blowing silica glass to make a vase.

Sulfur is a major ingredient in gunpowder.

Salt and Sulfur

The mineral halite is an important raw material. We get the chemicals chlorine and sodium from halite. The mineral sulfur is another important raw material. It is used to make **fertilizers** and insecticides for farmers, drugs for fighting diseases, and gunpowder.

ROCK SOLID FACTS!

FIREWORKS COLORS

Minerals help to make the colorful explosions we see during fireworks displays. When minerals with different metals are put in flames, they burn with different colors. For example, minerals that contain copper burn with a blue flame, and minerals that contain sodium burn with a yellow flame.

Grow Your Own Crystals

We know that many **minerals** are found as **crystals.** You can easily grow your own mineral crystals to see how crystals form in rocks. Here are instructions for growing crystals of two different minerals—halite (rock salt) and Epsom salts.

What you need:

- salt (rock salt, sea salt, and table salt all work)
- Epsom salts
- a kettle
- a liquid measuring cup
- water
- a teaspoon
- a clean jam jar
- a drink stirrer
- a paper clip
- thread

1 Ask an adult to boil some water in a kettle for you. Pour about 1½ cups (350 milliliters) of the boiled water into a measuring cup.

2 Put 2 teaspoons of salt into the water and stir until the salt has all **dissolved.** Repeat this step, adding a teaspoon of salt at a time, until no more salt will dissolve.

3 Carefully pour the salty water into the jar, leaving behind the salt that did not dissolve.

④ Cut a piece of thread about 4 inches (10 centimeters) long. Tie one end to the center of a drink stirrer and tie a paper clip to the other end. Put the stirrer across the top of the jar. The paper clip should hang near the bottom of the jar.

⑤ Put the jar somewhere that it won't be knocked over. Now you need lots of patience! Check the thread every day for crystals. After a few days, you should see small crystals growing on the thread. After a few weeks, you should be able to see that the crystals are small cubes. That's because halite always forms cubic crystals.

⑥ You can repeat the experiment using Epsom salts instead of table salt. This time simply put the jar of water into the refrigerator. After a few hours, you should see lots of needle-like crystals.

Glossary

conduct allow heat or electricity to pass through easily

crust thin layer of hard rock that makes up the surface of Earth

crystal piece of a mineral that has straight edges and flat faces

dissolve when a solid or a gas mixes with a liquid so well that it becomes liquid, too

element substance that cannot be broken down into simpler substances by chemical reactions

erosion wearing away of the landscape by flowing water, wind, waves, and/or ice

fertilizer substance added to soil to make the soil more fertile (so that plants grow better in it)

gemstone piece of stone that is valuable because of its beautiful color or pattern

geologist scientist who studies geology

malleable describes a substance that is easy to shape by hammering or bending

mineral natural, nonliving material found in Earth's crust

mineralogist scientist who studies minerals

organism living thing

particle tiny piece of a substance

property special quality or characteristic of something

sediment particles of rock that build up to make layers of sand, mud, or silt

Find Out More

Books

Oxlade, Chris. *Rocks and Minerals.* Essential Physical Science. Chicago: Heinemann Library, 2014.

Spilsbury, Richard, and Louise Spilsbury. *Minerals.* Let's Rock! Chicago: Heinemann Library, 2011.

Weidner Zoehfeld, Kathy. *Rocks and Minerals.* National Geographic Readers. Washington, D.C.: National Geographic, 2012.

Internet Sites

www.kidsloverocks.com/html/physical_properties_of_mineral.html
This website gives lots of information for kids about the physical properties of minerals, and more.

www.mineralogy4kids.org
This fun website is totally devoted to all things mineral! It also helps you identify the minerals in your home.

www.minerals.net/MineralMain.aspx
This database provides photos and descriptions of many different minerals.

Index